T0339365

THE PACIFIC NORTHWEST POETRY SERIES

Linda Bierds, General Editor

THE PACIFIC NORTHWEST POETRY SERIES

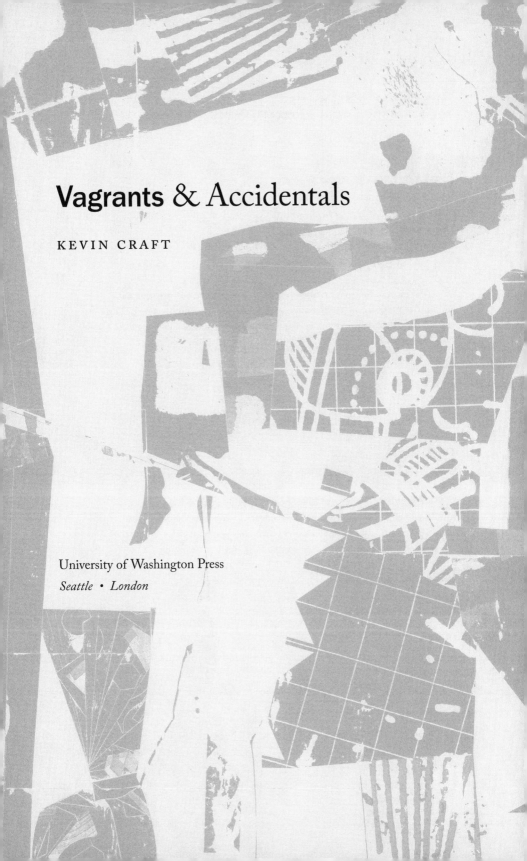

Vagrants & Accidentals

KEVIN CRAFT

University of Washington Press

Seattle • London

Vagrants & Accidentals, the seventeenth volume in the Pacific Northwest Poetry Series, is published with the generous support of Cynthia Lovelace Sears.

UNIVERSITY OF WASHINGTON PRESS
www.washington.edu/uwpress

Library of Congress Cataloging-in-Publication Data
Names: Craft, Kevin, author.
Title: Vagrants & accidentals / Kevin Craft.
Other titles: Vagrants and accidentals
Description: Seattle : University of Washington Press, [2017] | Series: Pacific
    Northwest poetry series ; 17 | Includes bibliographical references.
Identifiers: LCCN 2016013237 | ISBN 9780295999845 (hardcover : acid-free paper)
Classification: LCC PS3603. R339 A6 2017 | DDC 811/.6—dc23
LC record available at https://lccn.loc.gov/2016013237

The paper used in this publication is acid-free and meets the minimum requirements of American National Standard for Information Sciences— Permanence of Paper for Printed Library Materials, ANSI Z39.48–1984.∞

for Carmencita: sing along

Virtually every multiple arrival of passerine and near-passerine vagrants from the west occurs following spells of prolonged westerly gales at mid-latitudes, associated with Atlantic depressions that cross from the North American eastern seaboard at high speed . . . . Many weather systems are fierce and fast moving enough to entrain and displace birds from their normal flight path. When a specific set of weather conditions are met, large numbers of migrating birds may be displaced in our direction.

—Alexander Lees and James Gilroy,
"Vagrancy Mechanisms in Passerines and Near Passerines"

The appearance on the page of a thicket of accidental
flats followed by a thicket of accidental sharps and
naturals tells the eye
as well as the ear of metamorphosis.

—Susan Youens,
Schubert's Poets and the Making of Lieder

Partir toujours partir
Courir à la renverse

—Pierre Reverdy,
"Les Buveurs d'Horizons"

Contents

II

III

IV

Vagrants & Accidentals

Little Big Chief

Bees buzz about like stray conversation:
white heather, red heather, gentian, phlox.

Arrhythmia in the gully of displaced rock:
lichen loosens the hardest tongue.

So remembers this summer, the warmest
on record—névé like bandages,

hemorrhaging light. Red algae, white algae—
now as ever the sea floor rises,

mountains become ocean and ocean sky
summit shark's teeth magnify. It goes

without saying. I count five volcanoes,
each one keeping its furious distance, not unlike

the day you were born—daughter I turned from,
two hands wide. Two hands heavy

as a narrow traverse. No motion in the boughs
of subalpine fir. For one day made

out of tireless silence, not the first
nor the last word, time.

Water stitches into granite.
I shout at the cliffs the cradle the falls

———

returns no aphorism, no lookout
below. Lower still, passing tense,

speedwell, larkspur warm to my absence.
Yours is a prism, scattering blue.

I

I have a daughter
But no child
    —George Oppen,
      "Of Being Numerous"

Vagrants

Above the house, helicopters circle
all morning, all morning
rattling the fuchsia bushes,

alarming the hummingbirds, shuffling and re-
sorting the paperweight sky.
Whose world is this anyway, *throp throp*?

My neighbor winces at the dogwoods,
unnerved, trying to read the pollen count.
In my view, that's the pure purpose trivets serve,

patterning dust, all morning,
all evening,
though my view has been narrowing

since time began. Look: past the vanishing point
to the right of the fire station,
a scrub jay pokes at my plump cufflinks.

I'm dressing for a wedding or waiting
for redress. Nor is a scrub jay
native to my wardrobe—must have been caught

in a freak summer storm. Call
and response: your letters task
the listlessness overcomes me

while helicopters hover ever louder
overhead. Will they catch the aging fugitive?
Is the freeway traffic wriggling free?

I keep my eye
on that piece of atmosphere,
that wormhole of pacific

jet stream pouring through my window
some mornings emptier than others,
ferociously calm, spiked with the long notes

of a varied thrush. There's nothing not
trivial about a crossroads. Wherever you are,
send word.

Borders without Doctors

Things fly out of our hands
People fly out of our hands

Our hands like kelp crabs
     in a tide pool of braille
          scratching at the sandbar
     pinching the air

Our eyes like anemones
     straining to see straight
awash in the backlash
          an ocean of thimbles
     straining the tide

Sea stars fallen
     by the armful the wishful
          dissolving in hindsight
sucking broad daylight
     out of the rock

Nothing we can't withstand

     Nothing we can hold onto
          daylight streaming out of our eyes
oceans falling out of our hands

     Trees leaning hard
against the sky

Drivers on their car horns leaning
      O cornucopia of stall and blunder
           We have made it this far without

a handhold this far
        without a hand
     people fly out of

People like oceans
      oceans like plastic hugging the rock

The Descent

There was daylight therefore we grew eyes.
There were grasses therefore we grew lungs.

There were speeches therefore we grew an earful.
There were speeches we grew wary of.

Word-wary. Will he nil he. Circumspect.
First the thing then its preamble.

The people shall go a-walkin'.
The people shall go a-courtin' by starlight.

Therefore we grew musical: every move
a meadowlark, every drink a drum.

Thirstier we grew tongues like swizzle sticks.
The history of ideas produced a cocktail umbrella.

Knives in the atmosphere, ice in the stone.
Therefore we grew calluses. Calluses grew lungs.

We knew a thing or two but they beat us to it.
They beat us into it. *What's the big idea* our fathers used to say.

Carousel

I am sitting
on the grassy shore
of Alcyon Lake

fishing for lazy carp
or waiting for fireworks
to embellish

twilight in July,
the bicentennial
darkness warming

to history like a shy
friend I am following
now to the train tracks,

drawn by the distant
clatter and whistle
with a fistful of pennies

to smash into medallions,
ovoid and weighty
as a lie. From the tire

swing my brother
falls and cuts himself
in the rusty creek,

a little bloodletting
we survive by leaping
from sand bank to gravel bar

running from the stones
we throw at yellow jacket
nests for no good

reason, the heat of summer
coiling in our brains.
Soon they will drain

the lake, cup by cup
of poison leaching out of
the lakebed until

the mallards flee
the carp disappear
the geese grow oblong

lumpy like clumsy
lovers with no better
place to make

love memorable, never mind
where a duck goes
when the water's gone,

when the decade
evaporates
like gasoline in sunshine

billowing
out of both arms
open like the whitewash

glare of a missed slide
out of which a man
comes walking all over

again, brushing his sideburns,
holding up a fish
that glitters like the only
life he knows.

The Changeling

Like beargrass
you've grown
tender tall,
light bulb bright.

You colonize
an alpine meadow
like a chain
reaction, like beargrass

sifting blindly
as it towers
out of granite's
shadow, nervous and fixed

as the speed of light.
Sweet catena,
then you are one
idea leading to lakeshore,

another through switchgrass
and disconsolation,
the cliff-face where I overheard
my heart's own

tattle. Call this
dizziness or trans-
mogrification—
the bird released

———

from burden, the soul
from solubility,
no small
amazement to one now

steeped in disappearance,
like that girl long ago who
unflinchingly picked
one strung flower too many.

Among the Cypresses (23 Remedies)

Cut them down
or plant them in long rows tiger-
striping a country lane, still they harbor
hangnail shades, sighs of the dead: so were said

to shoot up suddenly in the harshest soils,
unsolicited, like any bird sprung
from their useless fruit. Mourning tree,
says Pliny: dowry for a daughter. Make me

a poultice of leaves for the snakebite
riding my ankle like an angry tattoo.
For you who've gone missing
in the vertical shadow,

who knock hardhearted in the deadbolt trunk—
salvo or echo, some bystander rage: sing me
the password to your dumbstruck grief.
Ring true. For every year hollowed out

of blind disbelief
another swings on its axis like high noon's curfew—
an epoch of abscess,
self-immolation.

If we could take Pliny at his word,
follow the sweep
of Spartan shadow, trace hernia
and sunstroke to their forgone source . . .

———

But nothing comes of it
but miscalculation, nothing but axle-grease
and bean meal for the swelling of the testes,
laughter the keenest of medicinal gulls.

Yet here they linger by the harbor,
these cypresses, pressing whose lost
sailor cause? Watch them ravage a hillside
in Languedoc, bear the writ of mistral

whiplash, scour the sky of its least adieu.
To be topmast and sarcophagus both—
to guard every graveyard
with monastic glee: is that harm's way,

or no harm done? It's the slow motion
sickness gets you in the end—you born out of
a thousand narrow escapes, breath
too close to call. Spare me

the tapering apex, spare me the generous
wick, dear witness, green as a god
or a lie. What I wouldn't give—a long arm,
a longer leg—

                    to eat the wind out of goodbye.

After Caravaggio

1. Narcissus in Darkness

Where image out of blackness deepens black.
Where white of doublet sleeve doubles wave
on wave. Slack water, lack luster: shadow
pooling in the eyes' orbit like gravity
engraved. If only I look long enough.
If only I long enough look like he
looks, languishing in solubility—
lips parted at the dew point of a kiss.
One hand dissolving into handsomeness.
One hand stipulating sand, stipulating
calyx, fingertip to tip addressed like
braille, like frailty, the meniscus
of starry membrane dividing night from
night, floodlight from its imminent collapse.

2. Echo's Remarks

—deep end. Lack
dabbles in craving
like lust her lash, oh
vagrancy—
gone funny
eking crooked
loss out of volume, ditty
joining feckless

and menacing
as lips loosen, lately
dressed like
don't mention it—
might come
yet to apocalypse—

Carbon Copy

Your eyes sketch
cartoon quicksand
against the eyelid dark, dreaming
the long wait of funnel spiders,

the lineage of houses
ensnared with flies.
Blue simmers
up from the coastline—

the gulf far below
holding every breath as you
untangle a shy Madonna
from acres of mummified wood.

Bread knife on the night stand.
Ceiling fan humming
it takes one to know one
to no one we know.

Uphill a dog barks
so insistently
pine trees spring from its mouth.
They stumble and angle

down a steep slope
as if tripping themselves
to take root in the act
of falling. Even at this

morning hour cicadas make
quick work of their limbs.
What's left is embarkation.
What's left is background

noise—static from that time
first words were uttered,
when unlikeness
opened our eyes.

Utilitarianism

A meal worm makes
a tinfoil moth.

People move through the sky
with electrifying calm.

Some of us stay up
all night unpacking crates

in supermarkets.
For others sleep

is the only exercise.
My knees ache

when I bend them past
the breaking point.

My elbows cross
to the other side of the room.

Who can say how a funnel
cloud funnels, or cakes,

or vacuums up
a choreless childhood day?

Who's that coming down the pike
with an ancient telegram?

The flagstones hardly
lift their heads.

Fluttering is for old flames.

Cycladic Head

Its one task is keeping
thought to itself, *tabula*
rasa, the blank slate raised
from stone to stare, gleaming
like a polished cloud,
a prism retracting
its rainbow speech, dumb-
struck and shapely
as an unstrung lyre—

And thus in being
stone sees, as a blind woman
knows feeling from afar
the rinse of starlight, her shadow-
white nose a gnomon, the first
distinction, mouth an erasure,
convexity of eyes like repealing
sky— O *anthropos*, lift
your chin, uncross your arms,

look up to me
from that ground you scour
with swollen belly and broken
bones, loam in which you tally up
love and loss alike— No more
than a paint fleck my last
look at you, beholder, shedding
limelight though you outstare
time itself

Les Calanques

Night by a window, the shifting
surf, wind trying all the latches.
Listen up: can you hear the ground

glass of telescopes scrying
like ropes in the rigging
of a sloop drawn taut? You must

know the universe is constantly
expanding. It's gritty inch-work
on the fast frontier. My watch

resembles nothing less
than the genius of happenstance.
I pass the hours

counting the days, pillaging the abacus
of what-ifs and wherefores.
The lighthouse flashes its tacit approval.

The lighthouse flashes at three removes.
Long before dawn
some kind of swimmer

detaches himself from shore,
the pebble beach seething, sharp-
tongued in the purple dark, eating

word for word each toothy wave.
Shutters strain against their
bronze age stays. Now the urchin divers

are stirring on the quays, mapping out
spiny constellations. The poem of daybreak
begins to write itself again

in limestone fissures. In it bison and ibex
stumble out of the cave, steaming
in torchlight, grazing their way

to the now distant coast. Behind them
in outline a hundred hands waving—
one of which must be yours.

The Weir

To catch an eel, pile stones in a shallow part of the river
to form a chevron wake of cackling geese gathering up switchblades and
    barb wire
to carve a violet furrow across the exile sky,
evening sky which you must assemble out of various drop cloths

and unwritten letters, not like the morning sky which is ready wear,
or the river itself which you must wring out of prehistoric tears.
Even the night must eventually be hauled up out of the cellar and stapled
    to its moon,
a few trees coaxed out of the ditches they had fled to

to escape human indifference and cruelty,
the stark kind manufactured in filibusters and centrifuges,
yes, also the playground version which is hand-me-down and haplessly
dangerous to saplings. Once the drones are launched,

once the wire laid across the ocean begins
cranking out another ocean, once the shards of broken bottles
find the mouth of the river, eels awaken in their tunnel vision,
eels ripple into parts of speech like vowels in exit wounds.

Wilson's Warbler

I.

Tip of the skull cap, black
hole in a blaze of olive sunlight
scavenging among leaves,
scourge of insects on the fly—

there's one at my window
twitching like a weather eye—poll
of one sporting no opinion,
miracle of circumstance in May—

which is to say
how does he find his way to our backyard
year after year (reiterating
émigré) ransacking the lilac,

pillaging the mock orange—light
weight (six or seven grams)
precipitate of the Pacific
flyway come to call one day here

a wilderness (I am that I am)
only to disappear beneath his cursory cap
in sympathy with darkness
as with archives, trafficking in previous lives.

2.

On the 11th July

we could plainly perceive land from the mast-head; but a terrible gale
of wind blowing all night from the shore, it was Sunday before
we again had the satisfaction of seeing it, scarcely perceptible
through the fog; but a pilot coming on board, and the sun rising,
we found ourselves within the Capes of the Delaware—the shore
on each having the appearance of being quite flat, and one perpetual
forest of trees. About seven at night, having had a good breeze all day,
we cast anchor at a place called Reedy Island, where one of the cabin passengers,
and the first man who leapt ashore from the long-boat, was drowned
on his return to the ship. We arrived at Newcastle next day
about mid-day, where we were all as happy as mortals could be;
and being told that Wilmington was only five miles up the river,
we set out on foot through a flat woody country, that looked in every respect
like a new world to us, from the great profusion of fine fruit
that everywhere hung over our heads, the strange birds, shrubs, &c.,
and came at length to Wilmington, which is on the side of a hill,
about a mile from the Delaware, and may be about as large as Renfrew,
or perhaps larger.

3.
Disconsolate wren,
where do you begin again
counting down your next-of-kin?

Once the nest is robbed,
once you've dropped
your weaver's bobbin,

scatter every nom de plume
composing poems at the loom
to pull a baby through a sonic boom.

Words fly. The past is past repair.
Meanwhile, excesses of laissez-faire
burn verses in the public square

and blot a peddler's poor bequest
with incitement to unrest.
File a plea of no contest:

becomes a flycatcher
to unburden human nature
of its leaden nomenclature.

4.

Green Black-capped Flycatcher
neat and active little species
I have never met with
in the work of any European naturalist
inhabitant of swamps
several times seen in the lower parts
of the states of New Jersey and Delaware
Amidst almost unapproachable thickets
of deep morasses it
commonly spends its time
during summer
has a sharp squeaking note
nowise musical
legs and bill flesh coloured
crown covered
with a patch of deep black
iris of the eye hazel

5.

Expelled from the noontide nap
to pick at gnats, all nervous
nonchalance foraging in foliage,
living on a budget of traveler's luck:

so Alex Wilson came to Philadelphia—
journeyman weaver, silk peddler, sharpshooter—
biased, almost from infancy, by a fondness for birds.
I take his word for it. One summer

camping near the Great Egg Harbor River
our teachers devised a snipe hunt (aka wild
goose chase) we fell for wholeheartedly, band of eighth graders
running circles in white sand, mucking through

cedar streams mined with snapper turtles
and broken bottles, our sneakers soaked, ankles stained
with tannins. It was easy to see how little we knew,
how the heart would fool us, the pine woods full

of itself, the buzzsaw of locusts
no *locus amoenus* hazing the migratory skyline,
each of us already a biography in tatters—
warbler, plover, storm-petrel, snipe.

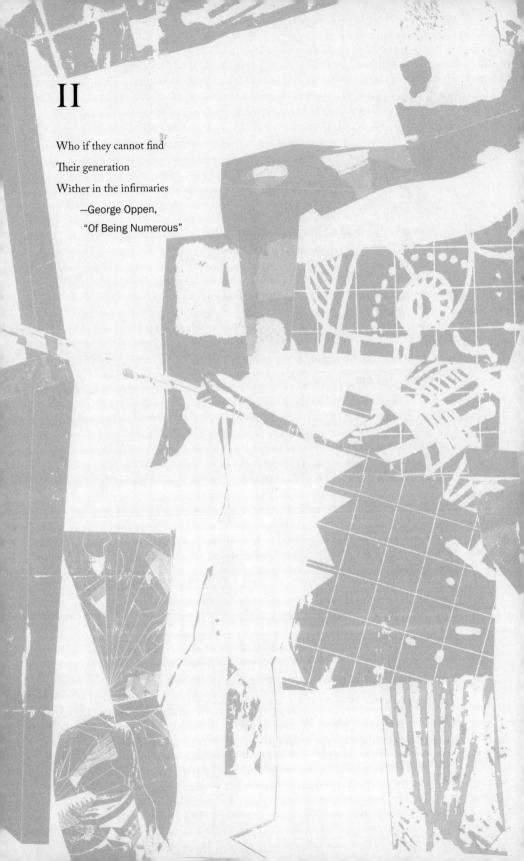

II

Who if they cannot find
Their generation
Wither in the infirmaries
—George Oppen,
"Of Being Numerous"

Matinee

She is one moving over the boardwalk—
my mother in Ocean City, New Jersey—crossbeam
hammered and hovering above the dune
line, boardwalk cracking like an exhumed spine.
So much love does she have for it walking
the boards has become her life's work,
measuring out the wooden miles like stalking
her own horizon, summer after summer
climbing down the gray-green ladder of the Atlantic
only to climb back up again, every plank a sleeper,
every nail a fraction of that solitude
named for the beach end of the road—12th Street,
13th—the music pier floating over breakers
like an ark. But who is alone walking
on a boardwalk if not my mother in winter
gauging the distance between storms
and the hours she has to make it through
childhood and back again, hers awash in
sistering, the small tasks of being eldest
among six, three in a room, one big bed,
born into a boom she can't escape.
I know her by the broad-brimmed hat,
the trail of gulls and the easy way
she lifts me from the splinter in my foot
or finds me somewhere in her twenties
sitting on a bench, waiting if not wailing through
a blank day lost and found. What do I know
about difficulty then except what I glean
from late night arguments in the kitchen,

my mother driving to work and my father
chain smoking at the end of the driveway,
never mind the hopeless weeping
she all but buries herself inside that summer
Christopher was lifted, blue and lifeless,
from the bottom of the pool. The Atlantic
has nothing on her, pounding out its names
for erasure, emptiness and fullness the same
calamity underwriting now the doo-wop band,
now the high school prom and string quartet,
drawing the sanderlings into its sheen,
chasing them aside. Through Cold War backwash
and every season of the Ferris wheel
she walks as if the boards depended on it,
the hardwood opening to her tender instep,
so many breaks collecting in her stride.

Untitled #10

Is that you looking over my shoulder Mark
Rothko looking like 1952 all over again the rainbow
harrowed prismatic glances shy like a planter's
bed a seeded cloud color seeping from your eyes
into mine Mark Rothko the halves and hues of a livelong

day is that you gliding through Cold War violets
the Red Scare and Bikini Atoll flashes to radical dust

let's get under our desks let's bivouac like Eisenhower
like ROYGBIV under the atmosphere the atomized beef
is that you in the bar code of spectral analysis you the iron
shine in an old sun's gut that's where it ends
where the photon perishes and we won't know it

for eight minutes more the light behind light's own
nuclear suffusion I see you everywhere Mark Rothko

in leaf sight and skydive swimming pool and switchyard
the eyes are the window of the eyes are the harrow
of pigment your witness your layer lament
we are close to overlapping our one mind divided
horizon your still life displacement your ground is there

a better self a clearer camouflage than plain
sight where the actuarial tables are drawn in our favor

the child still stuck beneath his linoleum shield
every day shadeless like shame in the blood
like a televised memory a blacklist I have touched
one or two radiant faces in my time hands
down this too shall be seen through and erstwhile

averted like a star hung nebula absolving all vector
the runway generation scattered in flight

Parents

My parents met in a supermarket.
He was an Acme checker with a black hair wave.
She bought Chiclets or ginger ale whenever she could.
It was New Jersey in summer, so they

were accompanied by a cloud of insects
wherever they went. They went to Margate,
Wildwood, Cape May. Kennedy and Khrushchev
warmed to their brinkmanship, their wing-tipped two-

step—not so my father. He bagged cucumbers,
lunchmeats, Wonder bread, smoked in the stockroom
on breaks. On breaks she was sorry to learn

about his father's failed heart. Now and then
I see her stop by the sweet roots and tubers
and hold them as if listening too long.

The Beardsley Limner

I.
I allow that I have trouble, you know,
being in the moment. I make to-do lists—
clean out the shed, begin reading Proust—
then go for a walk instead.

Not like Dr. Hezekiah Beardsley,
who's been occupying the same moment
of a clear spring New Haven day
since 1790.

There he sits sternly in his sparsely furnished
office, alone, while his patients—
the sons and daughters of Connecticut—
stand in ever longer lines

behind his door. He is not thinking
of the house calls that await him, the measles
and the whooping cough, he is stuck instead
on a sentence in volume two of Gibbons's

Decline and Fall of the Roman Empire—
some clause appalling and secretly thrilling,
something about Nero sneering or Diocletian
doing long division—

its meaning continually slipping
from his fingertips. Plainly visible through
an open window, Connecticut
levels out to green tundra

and a single poplar. I want to walk
toward that tree, a light wind off Long Island Sound
salting the air, while the sons and daughters
of the Revolution plow and till, bob and weave

or begin to study law, medicine,
while Hezekiah Beardsley sits pale and upright
in his green jacket, hand in chemise,
becoming the history he can only repeat.

2.
Suspended in her own moment, his wife,
Mrs. Hezekiah Beardsley, née Davis,
Elizabeth. She inhabits
a chartreuse gown the way a trapeze artist

inhabits a big tent circus. She has dog-eared
page 192 of the Reverend James Harvey's
Meditations and Contemplations, to which
she will return her undivided attention

once the painter has finished and I have
finally left the room. Behind her, a pink curtain
drawn to reveal a simple garden, red fern
and the camellia in bloom—*O Ye*

Flowery Nations—two stems
of which lie in her lap, while a white terrier
under the table stares up at her with that look
of unappeasable longing a dog can muster

on demand, and the fruit on the table—
a basket of apples and pears—hovers
in color between rose and flesh. Elizabeth
you are pale as the inside of a pear, your skin

a terrier's, your bonnet
a parachute, the doctor to whom you are
pledged a simple pendant
dangling against your bosom,

and though you have tired of this sitting,
of the portrait that kills you,
America remembers you with each generation,
America lies ahead of us, still.

Small Government

For instance, the sheen of headlights on a wet freeway
or a skunk hunkered in its burrow as the pinelands
shrink around it. Things exhibit de facto suffering
whenever you turn away from them, like that hammer
from your father's hand or the glass factory
sure of repeated blows from within. Turn back the clock,
the cloak and stagger. By now it's late,
too late for plate tectonics to save us from our lesser
natures, erecting cornfields between warring factions
or swallowing the acid rhetoric of an ocean,
any ocean with its plastic sheen and sinkhole interior,
its flotsam of made-in-China ducks and water pistols
loosed from a storm-knocked ship to circumnavigate
the globe at bath-time, little friend. What we have here
is a conspiracy against suffering, what we have here is
a declarative sentence with an election to swing. It takes
only two or three furnaces to turn the pinelands into
coke and/or whiskey bottles and/if gazing by an open window,
fewer the foundries of original intent. *Father, I lost*
the hammer and the appetite, it was I stole your cigarettes
your Buffalo nickels, we got Marathon bars for them
father, packs of Topps, mouths of smoke and gum . . .
Through which time the freeway thrumming, through which
loophole blue whales in their burrows, the glistening fenders,

quick glances lengthening in the windshield of tinted glass
because looking is a form of longing, in the end.
For instance, a blowhole, a sand flea, that silly putty smirk
you wear in the checkout line while having a nice day.
If not the stench of having rolled through county
after county awakening once more to its factory consent.

Flash Drive

—for Joe

Dreaming of blinders again
or drunk with that rage you carried
in a silver flask a permanent fiasco
riding your back pocket

you never saw the Mustang coming
T-boning the intersection
hugging the hairpin
turn of the horizon

dragging the highway into plain sight
all valves and rods, cones and pistons
backfiring into long dull basement hours
staring through the bottleneck

listening to The Smiths croon
How Soon Is Now
like steam leaking from a radiator
our own lives complicit in the clubroom

silence
the cassette tape rewinding
the cassette tape unspooling
as useless to the future as the future tense.

For the Climbers

Among the many lives you'll never lead,
consider that of the wolverine, for whom avalanche
is opportunity, who makes a festival
of frozen marrow from the femur of an elk,
who wears the crooked north star like an amulet

of teeth. In the game of which animal
would you return as, today I'm thinking
snowshoe hare, a scuffle in the underbrush,
one giant leap. You never see them
coming and going, only the crosshairs

of their having passed, ascending the ridge, lost
or not lost in succession forests giving way
to open meadow where deep snow
lingers and finally relents, uncovering
acres of lily—glacier yellow, avalanche

white—daylight restaking its earthly claim.
Every season swallows someone—
Granite Mountain with its blunderbuss
gullies, Tatoosh a lash on the tongue,
those climbers caught if not unawares

then perfectly hapless, not thinking of riding
that snowstorm to the summit, not thinking
wolverine fever in the shivering blood,
not thinking steelhead cutthroat rainbow
or the languid river that will carry them out.

Skunk Cabbage

Drain the future
languishing in fever
where a little
lavish sun-relieving
sunflower drowns
in excess of
sufficiency, suffering
not outlandishly
but lacking much too
muchness, headstrong
in meander, makeshift
in a shoehorn dream
of completion—how
far you are from
gleaning, earshot
cagey or conjugal
the argument
a garment
conceals, top hat
down and outer
wear, topiary charm
shoring up the
scenery, preening
like a lost
and found feeling,
freelancing forlorn.

Not Waving but Growling

Three feet into a surf-ringed
seastack, a puffin
excavates a burrow

to lodge its only egg.
Ten thousand puffins gather
to clear out half as many

discrete burrows in order to install
five thousand solitary eggs inside
this cliffside patch of North Atlantic turf.

Below and away surf batters
continental rock, the one sound
a puffin loves outright, muted now

inside the tunnel to an ambient roar.
After long absence, puffin parents
find each other by growl and bill,

hopping on the airy slope.
A puffin chick dispatched into this dark
earth alone, a single hatchling

wedged into a sleeve of grass and dirt
fills its bald belly with herring plucked
from its mother's rainbow beak.

The colony scatters in a great wheel
whirling above the perforated cliffs
to fend off poaching gulls,

even as, overnight, infinite stars
wheel in the feather dusted sky.
A puffin emerges from its peephole

to the broad brow beating of waves
ragged and familiar as one and the same
wave crashes in turn, each fledgling

made to scatter after dark
far out to sea for years on end alone,
solitary fish bird stitching

holes into the ocean. Clown-faced
prismatic flyer, little solitude—
riddle us now the face of the deep.

God: A Study

—after Raphael

Look, God's lost his flowing beard,
and like two-thirds of men on Earth is going
gradually bald—His head more egg
than planetary sphere,
a pendant penned in sanguine ink.

Just think
how He must feel, stripped of His locks,
robed in simple tunic, nothing
to blind the eye with, no lightning to scald
the less-than-shocked, the ever under-awed.

Senza aura, *senza* putti. He seems
a bit befuddled (if omnipresent
in His Loneliness) to have lived so
day to workaday, unmindful of the infinite,
distracted by the fray, nothing to show

for the big boom gone bust—
the continental drift, the monetary trust—
In God We—well, never mind. Is that a throb
rippling through His parietal lobe? *Mutatis
mutandis.* At least there's time to unwind.

If I confess I've seen God once or twice
in the usual guises—a hemlock
mobbed with mountain chickadees, the parted
silver dome of an observatory
faintly glowing at 1 A.M.—

shall I say God
is love of metaphor, *fiat lux*, a burning bush
those armies in the desert rush?
That's not to say God's a luckless
lover or a headstrong lead.

In Sanzio's cartoon study for the latest
Lamentation (in which colors
coalesce like freshest fruit) God's all washed
out torso on a grid—a downward nod
(is He asleep?), a gleaming lid—

and yet the care that painter entrusts
to palm and finger, the swift articulation
of the benedicting wrist
speaks beyond all rare command
of culpability, God the pulse and counsel near at hand.

On a Friday

A day like six coming up from the deep.
Little tongue wag, little tear of happiness.
Adam lifted from the dust.
Adam from paradise dismissed.

Not like Freya, distracted by finery.
Not like Venus born out of foam.
Revenue, ingénue, why so bleary?
Fish swim faster in the cold North Sea.

Cap the salt shakers. Don't break
fast. The harbor is thrumming, the ferry
undocking. Knock off early
where knock-offs last. And not least, the hangmen,

still on the clock, playing gruff games
with neckties and barstools.
You know the routine. You try thanking the gods.
Thirteen crows on a telephone wire:

they eat your words right out of the sky.

Finesse

With all the lost details,
you could have made a new world.
   —Pierre Reverdy, "Voyages trop grandes"

That spider that lived through winter
on your living room ceiling—a stationary dot.

Houseplants you didn't kill. Dates
you didn't keep. All the hand-drawn

suns and flowers you received
in kindergarten to commemorate your hernia,

your hospital stay.
That gone feeling of going under the gas.

The taste of chocolate milkshake
biting your tongue.

Winter that survived in the abdomen
of a spider, like a letter you write every day

in air. Flubbed lines at the audition.
In Marrakesh, a map of Marrakesh, the monkey

posing for a picture on your back.
More oranges. Fewer haircuts.

The words of the woman on the night train to Kiev.
The night train to Kiev.

Kiev.
Your password and whatever you changed

it to. This too shall pass into worldly possession.
Four tiny spiders that repopulated

the tundra of your ceiling. Filament of a letter.
The day you connected the dots.

Fuzz

When I think of him at four I think how
we would slip quietly
from the porch each morning before school

to see what the grass had washed up,
see those rabbits come out of the wood
feeding in half-light

on the unmown lawn. Among the wreckage
of tricycle and swing set
we could always count on two or three

waders, nibbling diligently, vigilant
as daybreak, their hunger
cut like wakes in the backyard shallows.

Each morning though our school bus exodus
sent them scattering, there was a pause
before we parted ways, a lifting

of noses, a tensing of ears just long enough
to amplify the gnawing in our own
amphibious hearts.

—*Christopher Craft, 1970–1974*

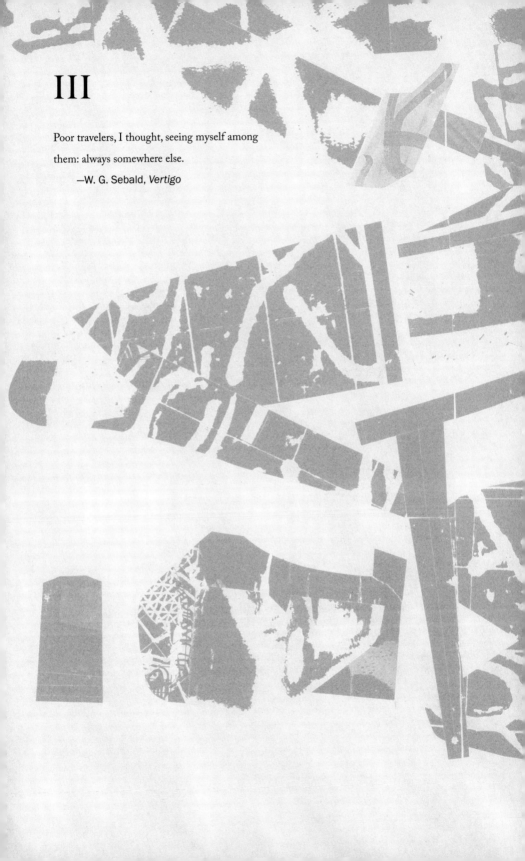

III

Poor travelers, I thought, seeing myself among
them: always somewhere else.

    —W. G. Sebald, *Vertigo*

Transparency

Years later (43) my father offers a name—says
I looked over the desk, saw the paperwork stray
when the caseworker ducked into the backroom—
says this casually, over the phone, in the middle of some
playoff talk about the Phillies or the weather in Florida,
recounts it as a known fact, something I must have
learned long ago, and forgotten, like the allegory
of the chariot pulled by two horses—tells me her name was
Madeleine, just like that—*I thought you knew*—
as if everyone in Wilmington, Delaware knew—
knew the circumstances, the chemical shame,
1967, the indelible fact of having gotten herself
pregnant by no name my father can recall seeing—
just Madeleine of the typescript, Madeleine
of the dotted line, Madeleine of the horse & buggy split.

*   *   *

I'm thinking 17, I'm thinking dropped out
of high school, sight unseen, I really don't know,
except in one iteration my name is *Michael*,
that I knew by 8th grade, at least, when Lori Wiedner
started calling me that, Lori the first flute,
Lori the perennial September crush who sometimes flirted
though usually not, though she would offer up
magnanimous middle school warmth and alarm
and thus in her eyes did I begin to live that other
boy's life as well as I could before the *World Book
Encyclopedia*—peeling back layers of see-through anatomy

to get to the nervous system—autonomous
if not sympathetic—the skeletal remains,
the blank page wavering behind it all—
I have been poring through your absence all these years
scratching out name after name

Linear A

I am the city
as you remember it,
save one.

I am a dark
incision—cat's eye or claw
in a field of slash and burn.

No sooner said than
waves will slosh
on a half-moon beach—
fond of their habit
and the leisure of five
wild swans.

(My rival's an archive
of miscarried fleece.)

Divulge what you will,
embryonic *kri-kri* swimming
circles around our knuckles,
gold goddess hovering
like a hornet
in a thumbprint epiphany.

Even stones
have pastimes—stepping down,
weighing in.

———

Now hindsight flickers like a bull's
bright horn
cleared by a headlong
running leap.

(We're beginning to tabulate
our livestock in dreams.)

When summer
fills the lustral basins
with green water, terrapins
ringing the cistern

like a loose archipelago—
when the whole
sluggish island nose-dives
like a foundering whale—

I am the ladle they call
Diaspora,
I am the rhyton
whose measure is tears.

Drink up. Wish me luck.
(Cuttlefish thrash in a whirlpool cup.)

So that blue monkeys swing
in turpentine trees,
so that blue women
chatter like chickpeas in jars:

———

all the figs of Memphis
are not sweeter than your fingertips—
so long out of touch, so long out of touch
they trace their lineage in scar.

Persona Non Grata

I wore a mask made of holes,
none of which weep. I was armed
like a gladiator to face assimilated sheep.

I could only nod or shake, never blink,
never strike like a bowling ball
in a back alley brawl. I was a chain letter

composed of missing links. It wasn't my style
to menace or gloat.
Here's what I learned: like a bowling ball

tossed into the drink, half of us sink
and half of us float. Which is why it took so long
for Shelley, billowing in Ligurian troughs,

to wash up on a Pisan beach.
He had to have it both ways, coursing
off course, whereas I rode out of town

on my own stalking horse. Archimedes
sank into his Syracusan bath
and came out the other side, thin

as a meniscus, having moved the Earth
with javelin shade. He did the math,
but still this could not save him

from a Roman soldier's blade. Likewise, Ovid
in a Black Sea arcade. How do you translate
solitary confinement?

Jade is rarely prized among the jaded,
carnelian among the Gorgon's foes.
Imagine, for the first time, those follicles

writhing, those sutures erupting
with tectonic woe. When only rivers
balk and cry, ask another banished hero

to look her in the eye. (Not every tear's
a crocodile lurking in the Nile.) Like a masquerade,
coastal Campania is riddled with caves.

My descendants are the gawkers and gapers
of Neapolis, the fumaroles and forked
tongues of Phlegraean fields who haven't lost

their touch so much as fled
to cigarettes and convertibles
in Nyack, New York. They know

---

the secret stares of peacocks, the audible
of the pass rush, the vigilance of thunder.
They know the prescription

for ancient hangovers: seven laps
around the gridiron, one for every sage
or wonder. One Mississippi, two Mississippi . . .

the underworld holds nothing new.
Believe you me, I wore myself out
trying to escape from view.

On Turning 38 in Rome

Long ago you outlived Keats
and even your early reading of Keats.
Now if there were more than water
to your name
and nothingness to secure your fame,
you might sip a glass of claret
with the beggars in the streets.
Milestone or millstone? Why decide?

Meanwhile, back to homicide
and another unsinkable comparison:
like La Barcaccia entered in regatta
33 came and went
without stigmata.
And this year in the Pantheon
you bent
over backwards respecting ocular heaven
and Raffaello of Urbino
who quit this earth at 37.

Now, here in the Campo Marzio
where soldiers lay their arms to rest
you try your chiaroscuro best
to outlive Caravaggio. No,
not with brush and not with gun
but in the glower of the sun
where worse than lizards have it made,
and you, fighting for a wedge of shade,
shouting, "Tennis anyone?"

New Volunteer at the Art Museum

One could hold up a leaf as a fine example
of yellow's exacting workmanship.

The world goes about its business thus
and thus, I watch another hour chase

frisbees in the park. I say *miniature*
where you say *confide*. The clouds come

loping and we lower our voices, as in greenhouses
where the deserts of the world

go on expanding. Who doesn't love
a jade pagoda, a cactus wren? But on the edge

of a shallow dish I'm mystified. Ungainly,
shapely, the shadows of camels accumulate mass

beneath the shadows of gilded crows.
Behind closed doors, a gallery of Buddhas

goes on smiling. I know that if I grab your hand,
the Song Dynasty period will begin again.

Nisqually Delta

Mid-winter, two egrets
inaugurate a marsh
standing maypole-still—

thin as saplings, thinner
than rain, deliberate
as arrows strung in a bow.

See how easily they are two
of a kind, twice upon
a time, mindful not so much

of each other as of
any movement
in the river,

the slowness of the river
dividing each egret
from its likeness

and the river itself
reaching the end
of its tributary life, doubling

and redoubling
its opaque
meander, mudflats

brimming, egrets
angling, glaciers gathering
force upstream.

Lignum Vitae

—Galleria Borghese

Caught mid-stride, taproots, tendrils shooting down
from tripped toes like a mangrove straining
an estuary, no part of Daphne
touches ground,

the downfall of her right foot loosening
its ferocious calf-climbing bouquet of shade,
her midriff trailing a bonsai glade
which entails her pursuer, pierces his groin . . .

As sudden as a gust pales the poplar
against encroaching sky, so he palms her waist,
a look of bewilderment entering his face
as his fingers find not skin but scar.

From the blind side they've fled into abstraction,
gone into the grove of themselves
to hang on as vortices, *selva*
oscura, a gnarled old thick-boughed oak ingrown

with worry, age-blunted rage, the tree of life resealed.
Spun out of windblown cape and cross-purposes—
the girl she was, the man he couldn't be
a simple stone, a garnish of leaf at his heel.

Linear B

I've etched each phoneme
of your name into this
my most beautiful vase.
Some seal their *kraters* with poly-
chrome fire, others with a kiss.

And so it goes with octopuses
whose beaks can crack a mollusk;
who, startled, release
quick clouds of ink, escaping
into self-made dusk.

Beyond the sinkhole
of love and fame, I've no more
reliable appliance.
I dally in the harbor, daubing
starfish on faience.

Count your figs and figurines.
Secure the harried latch
to the storeroom whose great *pithoi*
mock our losses, love. If only
we could start from scratch.

Carmen Saeculare

Would there were a way to turn this slow
heat rising off Roman cobbles into the hail
it wants to be falling on your doorstep,
love, just before we step out to load the car
drive from Seattle over the mountain
passes to the channeled scablands in spring
where evidence is ice breaking all over
again like the great dam bursting into flood
and if Lake Missoula remains a puzzle
only basalt remembers clearly beneath
migratory waves of Canada geese the hieratic
scrawl of sandhill cranes still there was no
getting out from under it like this heat
spiraling off the Piazza della Pace
into which swifts throw themselves with sheer
abandon cutting broad swaths of it and presto
a parasol opens above another
aperitivo into which a man peers
as if looking for a coin he dropped a contact
lens a magnifying glass on the pointillism
of some bulbous *bucchero* vase an artisan of Caere
took great pains to punctuate with radiant
fans like stiletto peacocks like sunrise
on Pluto like a third cocktail umbrella
through which I drink beside a stranger in honor
of your absence which is fondness personified
and the soft spot behind your left ear where
the boundless first flared (like that strain
in stranger) and dampness bifurcated fire

---

the way Anaximander described it
in Ionia long ago Ionia the enlightenment
smuggled in the fluting of columns
the contraband spun in the rigging of masts
the subtending thump loosed from an upright bass
accompanying accordion in the piazza this evening
plying through "My Way" for the umpteenth time
followed by the *primi piatti* followed by
"Those Were the Days" which the cobbles could play
with their eyes closed and sometimes do
though no one in the Dark Ages ever painted night
I go walking *molto andante* from piazza to piazza
holding myself up like a sputtering torch
until the heat applauds the accordion collapses
the upright bass lurches over the pedestrian
bridge and so it goes trying to swim
beneath Dry Falls or wash your hands in Ancient Lakes
and though I say *io io io*
I mean that owl that all night signals from
basalt cliffs as the fire dies and you crawl
into your sleeping bag and the bassist lays down
his mortal frame and I slip in beside you
wave crumbling into wave.

Parakeets in Rome

At first I didn't know what I was seeing.
There was one at the museum

for Etruria, carousing like an alarm clock
in the solitary pines, though it lacked

an interlocutor. Might have found a ready one
among the glazed ducks, or those smiling iron

figurines Etruscan smithies forged
to signify that no matter how dark the age

some kinds of happiness endure. Happiness and terror,
to be sure, not to mention trial and error,

and territorial dispute.
(But that point's long since moot.)

Among those squint-eyed, black robed, tippling augurs
ubiquitous as weekday bloggers,

a word, favorably disposed, might have been heard
rising into the canopy, credentialing this bird

auspicious. Each time it flapped, flashing wings
and dragging its forked tail like green lightning

from pine to pine, I cocked my ears.
Could parrots learn to parrot ancient seers?

Naught but squawking came down, in return,
to call that dead heat race around an urn

where every proffered omen springs a leak.
But O for a smattering of Etruscan from its beak!

And the eager silence? That was still mine.
I hoofed it over to the Palatine

where, days later, sure enough, another
stray was searching and/or screeching for its brother.

We know that story well—too well. Before it reached its crisis
I left that blazing bird to its devices

and found myself strolling, *ambulo ergo sum,*
on the far side of the Janiculum—

Villa Doria Pamphilj. It was morning.
Joggers, mountain bikers, picnickers galore

would soon arrive, but for now—never manic—
dawn had washed the slip off its ceramic

sleeplessness and, rose-fingered if not horse-drawn,
was spilling centuries of daylight on the lawn.

The park is many landscapes
folded into one: woodland, meadow, escapades

of fountain dribbling into weedy lakes; soccer
pitch; olive grove; acres of manicured

hedge and rose—in a word, Eden,
recreated for the postmodern

exurban lifestyle, which Rome has been past fashioning
for ages now that it has spread like a rash

across the biosphere. Did I say rash?
That was—inhumane. I meant thrash—

as in thrashing, as in parakeets, of a sudden
moving through the trees—dozens

of them—like a string of ill-timed sneezes
departing with the souls of whom-it-pleases.

These were not geometers in laconic
poses proofing outlines in the pines' Platonic

shade, mere afterthoughts
of umbrellated architecture, starkly wrought.

This was a real invasion.
As I stood there, gawking in amazement,

several thoughts occurred:
are these descendants of that lisping bird

for which Ovid penned a dirge,
vox mutandis? The metonymic urge

of jungles staking out a future claim?
Nature hardly answers to the name.

———

Once out of Eden . . . said and done.
Meanwhile, Pangaea rushes to reconstitute in London,

Sydney, Istanbul, Madrid.
We watch sub-Saharan forests shrink, aridity

encroaching like a lidless eye,
while escapees of the bird trade multiply.

Not to mention snakes—enterprising garden arbiters—
pythons squeezing panthers out of Florida.

Invasive species? We should know,
and pride ourselves on saying so

without chagrin, suspending disbelief
that willfulness could ever come to grief.

Willfulness or wilderness—the day grew hot.
Those parakeets seemed to know their lot:

part torpor, part arrow,
scattered like a deck of tarot

cards against a drooping sky—
giving paradigms of paradise the lie,

alternately bellicose and brooding,
like a bruise,

originally imported to amuse.
And if they held their tongues like talking statues

———

still the word got out:
call it mystery, uncertainty, or doubt,

I watched them cling to it, vanish into its uppermost
reaches, until one gasp, one raspy riposte

brought them storming out of the canopy
again—all hoopla

and enthusiasm brandishing disclaimer,
a god by any other name, or

close enough.
The language isn't made of finer stuff.

The Quagmire

If the art of shipbuilding were in the wood,
we would have ships by nature.
 —Aristotle, *Metaphysics*

You may laugh as matchsticks
sprout up out of spark;
that galleon growing in my yard
was once a little barque.

A bowsprit made of splinters,
from chopping blocks a stern;
how can you trust your fences
with much mending to unlearn?

A poem sleeps in paper,
yes, a crows-nest in the stars,
a soldier makes his lonely name
fighting other people's wars.

The quarries spit out statues
of enviable men
just as quagmires require auguries
to distinguish egg from hen.

A feather's tickled speeches
take winds out of a sail—
he travels hard and farthest
where the predicates prevail.

———

I'll go with you to Bedlam,
love, I'll follow you to bed;
the children of indifference
turn luck out on its head.

From money, ready profit,
from calendars, quick time
to conjure up experience
in punctuated brine.

From quantum leap to quarter rest,
sad music emanates
from ears attune to deafness
no silence penetrates.

Yes, you may flinch as matchsticks
blossom out of fire
and scratch out every consequence
we make of our desire.

The ocean widening in my yard
was once a little fissure:
a shoulder blade, a pinch of salt
thrown backward for good measure.

Bivalve Lullaby

I used to think they lived out
their shuttered lives wherever they happened
to spin fast and spawn—blue mussels shagged on pilings
striped with seaweed, wedged in the crevices
of breakwater jetties—great shocks of them
exposed at low tide, seething like a janitor's keys.

Or take the oysters quiet in their beds—
a thousand siestas filtering oceans
to map out a dollop of nacreous glamor
one could die for, diving—now dissolving in acid
like any reckless tongue. You'd be forgiven
for guessing the geoduck's a geyser, an inter-
tidal spitting contest stuck in mud—
and every clam dragging its foot from door to door.

So when I first see how at the lightest touch
scallops leap up from the seafloor like madcap castanets
carrying the fluted claptrap casing of themselves
through bandwidths of eelgrass, straining the water column
like an erratic heartbeat—

I am dumbstruck
as in that other dream when the body, hard of hearing,
takes flight, unreeling as matter and gravity
come unhinged, the polarities of attraction
reversed. How long until mackerel
spill out of cloudbanks, or castaway
oceans bring down the moon?

They are beautiful in propulsion,
scallop shells radiating displacement—
lop-sided, hangdog, all grin-and-bear-it eyes for teeth,
vision's own benthic bursts plucking away
at the bubble wake abyss—wobble and pitch—
like the butterfly strokes of infant swimmers
riding a raft of quicksand notation, some accidental
melody released into solution, free-
wheeling, tide-spun, gone.

Low Hanging Fruit

The washing machine shrieks
like three howler monkeys fighting in a forest canopy.

It's a lazy dispute—
something about breadfruit not native to these parts.

Outside it isn't raining. Inside the girl sleeps
to the row of monkeys hissing

among territorial leaves, beating their fists
against the broken boughs. Maybe she likes

the rhythm. Maybe she dreams of the jungle
she grew out of—rosewood, kapok, little violin.

I am upstairs noticing
everything that hasn't happened:

stunt pilots climbing out of biplanes,
media junkets gathered on the lawn.

Maybe it takes a sleeping girl
to underscore the incivility.

Soundbites of howler monkeys
ravage the neighborhood.

Outside loop, hammerhead stall.
Always the heavy waiting in the wings.

———

IV

Time passed, and some of it became this.

—Louise Glück, "Landscape"

Old Paradox

Consider that a single grain of sand
cannot be arranged so as to form
a heap.

Consider that it's difficult
if not impossible to discover the exact
moment a tadpole becomes a frog,

the precise instant *al dente*
loses its bright tooth. At noon I am
half in love with you, half distracted

by the dishes in the sink.
Now the soul: tell me where is it
that split-second before

and after the old woman who is mother
and grandmother and cousin
to those assembled in a hospice room

kisses her own immigrant grandmother
on the cheek as she leaves that Napoli
she left long ago

forever in the past? In dying, does she
take the flyswatter with her,
does every cell turn off at once?

One death permeable as grief,
another obdurate: they lean against
each other, accumulating

mass. On a scale of extravagant
to frugal, we fall everywhere
between.

Accidentals

1. *Figure of Aeolus*

They found you under twenty feet
of loose ash—sirocco-pelted,
ozone-haunted—one vowel
solo in an archipelago

of strung-out vowels and doting volcanoes—
Isole Eolie—O hoop
of exhilaration, sigh of relief
softening your votive mouth

if not blowing off steam
at the crater rim, crystalizing sulphur,
poring over tomes, the trade winds
and furies that fan through your realm—

citizen-king, O sonorous persona
weaned on fumes and that old
itinerant intonation—air
your woes all over again—

2. *Villa dei Papiri*

Scroll down: at half an inch an hour
it took Piaggio's machine four years
to unravel Book 4 of Philodemus's
treatise *On Music*: a score

of harmonies unheard for centuries
wrapped in scorched papyrus, one
of thousands stacked in a library
buried by Vesuvius, palimpsest

of pyroclastic flow. One touch
turns the seared word to ash, and so,
patient reader, Piaggio constructed
his machine to open slowly,

clockwork letterpress churning
in reverse, revealing its charred text
line by line—cowlick of coal dust
and carbon copy dating

extolling the pursuit of pleasure
in the subtraction of pain—
the texture of sound *in absentia*
singed to a cinder cone pith—

a blacksmith's art, to be sure,
forgery of atoms we turn to X-rays now
to disentangle torch from song, marking
what "would fall" "would say."

3. *The Only Moving Thing*

And then it was raining blackbirds
by the flock, Arkansas a panic of sky
spitting out blackbirds, pummeling
the tarmac of a New Year's midnight—

blackbirds falling for no reason
anyone could put a finger on—
four score and twenty score, acres
of augury gone south in a hurry—

red-winged blackbirds like unexploded
ordnance darkening driveways,
deafening meadows, dead aim
taking flight, leave-taking—

the sky a riven thing
hammered into chimneys, a vacancy
Averno-like in its buoyancy
grounded—wingless or godless the fumaroles

fire and its fallout procure
in that "place of no birds"
where the Anthropocene first set foot—
prophecy of self fulfilled.

Entanglement (Sombrero)

Crows on the roof ransacking rain gutters
I have to learn to say things straight out to be
birdbrained is both frivolous and sharp
I know that much not to beat around the bush
except when that's useful perhaps when the bush
is burning next to your house and I want to save you
from the cigarette left next to the bed your mother's
catatonic gin your father's face red like
the animal knowledge of kerosene creeping through
a Russian novel and if the cosmonaut abandons
ship? What's a monkey wrench in orbit? What's a bar
of soap drifting past the Kuiper Belt when God
is everywhere and also nowhere there is
darkness in all matter brother between you and me

I like it that way. Which is not to say
crows on the roof are frivolous or dizzy.
That summer the arsonist took out a dozen houses
three restaurants and a society of classical guitars
the entire neighborhood slept uneasily you couldn't
light a cigarette without catching someone's eye.
I thought of Rilke's flamenco dancer
stamping out each flame become the blaze
in the Olive & Grape that nearly destroyed the theatre,
and the joke was shouting theatre! theatre!
to the firemen in the street. The crows took notes
as ever they caught the guy some drifter
with a history of kerosene on his breath. Darkness
orbits your heart dear sister like a hat.

Core Sample

After moat-clearing or spring insurgency
or the walk around the sinkhole block
comes ecstatic tapping of the flicker
clocking fresh hours on a telephone pole.

Even our silences are territorial—*not here
not here.* The tar pits of La Brea in the news:
paleontologists reconfigure another cache
of Ice Age bones sifted from synoptic ooze—

dire wolves and arthritic mammoths
whose ribs had broken and healed, a loose
compendium of ground sloths and bison
the bog had swallowed whole.

I have noticed that all my walking
has had little effect on these streets
whose condemned houses lean
into the maw of the underground creek.

On the long path through the park, first I see
the girl-child hanging on the hands of her parents,
then a mile down the trail her dropped hat.
Tonight they will wonder where it went.

Some things don't want to be found—like a fork
rephrasing silence. Before the dazed animal eyes
of certain industrial landscapes, switchgrass
and towering fern, the flickering of ice.

———

Therefore Wander

That cabbage moth fluttering
like loose ends or an old itch in the vagus

nerve finds the underside of a spirea leaf
to cling to

at the garden end of a windy
day—and then? Long night.

Let's not worry about plot.
Restlessness carries you

from leaf to leaf, the moon shines
on your deeds, good

and bad. To investigate what's at stake
for a moth scrawling its nervous

syllogism from porch light to candle
and back, carrying the singe

of proximity with it,
approximating the breadth of the material

world in its stark
abandonment of principle, its even

underhandedness, requires no scapegoat,
no backstory

of blindness and scorn to cut through
to the inevitable

avalanche, the white-out conducive
to moving through fog

to figure grounded in fog
to disfigurement. Each time

I hold out my hand,
you escape.

Entanglement (Satellite)

1.
It's hard to believe these mountains.
From *Mariner 10*, 1974
is a planet undeterred by speed.

Ghost craters. They speak
the dialect of future remission—
bl/ink, curs/or, gap/e.

That was great, said the future.
That was then, said the West.
Returning to the issue of wolves.

Still, mountains make good movies.
Slow & lo were we
flying when we reached the lake

2.
the end. Cattails.
Satellite glide path, inkling.
A vapor surrounds us. Toward.

3.
Up from the sea bed
a fish wriggles out of
medieval schools.

We bury him today—
monkfish, namesake.
The soil as he knew it—

blowflies. Eggs of the apple snail.
Strings of snow geese
for a splintering

4.
family tree. The sisters rise,
arm in arm. The eldest standing
to one side: calls for the interpreter.

Stars rush past their
starving light. It's our turn
to eke out a living.

Pigeon Guillemots

Dangle bright red legs
floating and diving
like simple sentences
by the ferry terminal—

so close, and closing in—
their glide paths trimming
acrobatic pilings,
rounding off the long division

of the tide. Spring: Saturday
opens a beer and passes it
around. Dear sunlight,
we missed your clean throw rugs

beating on the bay.
There's no place to get to
but we're going anyway.
Guillemot—like *guile*,

only less so, a bon-mot
waiting to lodge itself
in your bailiwick.
Compact. Glossy.

The world still has a thing
or two to show us,
much of which passes
for guillemots today.

———

The Break

When you were two
we played the game of peekaboo,
only you called it *on dort par terre?*

And so we feigned sleep
on the parquet floor assembled
like a pictureless puzzle beneath

our sleepyheads, and roused
ourselves mere seconds later singing
il faut se lever! to the stilted air.

No place seemed too far away
for chasing pigeons, or trouncing puddles
in a park, or listening for the odd

toss and dull thump of balls landing
where the old men played *pétanque.*
And so a late summer of loose

heartbeats passed, one knocking the other
closer to or farther from the target
cochonnet. When pigs fly

I will show them the way
back and forth across the North Atlantic
with its toy ships and ragged coastlines

and blue whales never breaking through
the surface of our sleep.
For years I spoke to you in dreams

which took place in rooms
furnished like a Neolithic plain—
menhirs dropped into a field,

legions of them frozen in formation
from Carnac to Corsica,
stranded like no stone unturned

in extravagant alignment,
stelae gripped by grin-and-bear-it,
together and alone.

How does a bluethroat
dress for an apology so deep it's grown
its own appendages, a stillness like no other

drawing breath? And what have you become?
I wrote letters like paper airplanes
thrown against a mâché sky.

Some words we chew on so long
they weld themselves like barnacles
to the tongue. *Otter, spotter,*

daughter, solder goes one rhyme
scheme I carry under my tongue
like a coin for every ferry. When you were

sixteen I waited beside a merry-go-round
in Montpellier, afraid I might not recognize
your face, which came to me

across the pebbled promenade
like a hall of mirrors.
Of all the ways a life can break

this was strangest: *Je est un autre*
I read once in a hellish book.
And what has I become?

You didn't have to take a second look.
No failure's more familiar
than all the things I could have done

to write a different ending, but didn't,
gripped by some paralysis
of a parallel universe

in which loosened
moons come crashing through the ceiling,
and one of us rises

to wake the other, to shake
the sleeping earth to its core,
just an ocean knocking at the door.

House Finch in Bird Bath

Down through backyard dogwood
and apple tree a dabble of red
dropped from the telephone wire

to splash in the shallow dish
of his quick reflection, flicked wing
on wing stirring things up,

trimming and combing the ruffled
tail coverts with conscientious
glee, but briefly, returning

to the singing wire fast
as he left it, whistle wetter, brighter
the bristled crimson cap and bib

rising from his self-
inflicted bloodbath like spark off flint,
a tassel of slash and burn.

An Illustrated Guide to Feathers

1. *Flight Feather*
At the beach a tall tree had acquired a parasail. We began by looking up.
The wind began by returning the favor.

2. *Contour Feather*
We turned a corner. We turned down the job offer in Oklahoma. We
turned out in large numbers. We turned page after page in the guest book
looking for a place to turn in. Things grow round in filtered sunlight.

3. *Semiplume*
Clouds had gathered at the watering hole. There was some pushing and
shoving. There was some posturing and pasturing. Then everyone broke for
the nearest speech balloon.

4. *Down*
Sleeping bags of America, rise up!

5. *Bristles*
He seemed like a nice person
is no way to live.
These dishes will not break themselves.

6. *Filoplume*
Wind speed. Speed date. Date palm. Lamprey. Pyre.

Hard Return

The window.
The wild.
].
The weird wonder at the way things rise.
The slow   down.
The incomplete.
The make-up work, the lack [of exercise.
Of exercise: Lift. Run. Spit.
[Repeat.]
The nail polish.
The next-of-kin.
A little less than.
The number of times I said *A*.
The number of times you said *B*.
The jump-start.
The jump-ball.
Jubilation. The
the lie.
Solving for *X*.
Solving for why not *Y*.
Not I.
The way things take care of themselves.
The way selves take care of themthings.
The weird wonder.
The slide.
The lack of.
The wind.
O, the fiction it portends.
C'mon now.

———

The [emendation].
The allowance.
The amends.

The Undertow

I know only what the towhee knows,
its dry buzzing a blown fuse, short circuit
chiseling wet grass. A little bourbon goes
a long way in this daydream I plagiarized
from a skiff in the harbor, a little meaty
effervescence in the unsound sky.
That all day float planes drone overhead
like sawmills has nothing on the glitter-faced
magician's assistant surviving blade after
blade hacking through her open casket, except
where the sky cuts her clean in two. Out pour
the rattlesnakes, out pour the howler monkeys
swinging through alleys like telephone wires.

I'll take her word for it any old day
who shadows the bluegrass quartet from city
state to state, caught in the undertow, adrift
in the intertidal surge. Voices shatter
over the harbor, voices over water carry laughter
a long way from its source. Every fall vine maples
make a great show of their religion.
Comb jellyfish climb the ladder of being
the way a daydream splinters down the spine.
How to bridge the distance between howler
and human is a problem for the pine trees now.
Out go the lights, wildfire consuming the prairie.
Out go the luminescent tides.

One Atmosphere

I do my part
to hold up one loose end of it,
to shoulder my spoke of the beanpole sky
which keeps falling
heavily on me some days
loaded up like a straw
full of camels, some days lighter
like a needle's eye
but on average measures
65.4 Newtons per square inch
pressing like the weight
of the shirt off my back,
no more than a backpack
stuffed with asterisks,
in fact, or a basket of starfruit
I balance on my head
walking from room to room
alone in my house or standing moderately still
at the periphery of a cocktail party
not unlike a weather balloon
or a telamon
in a graduation ceremony
or one of those upstanding women
on Attic vases
or in African deserts
or Mesoamerican jungles
with perfect equipoise
portaging great water-jars
from well to village

transporting a river off the top
of their heads
only for me so much easier to bear
like euphoria
like the ritual enthusiasm
that grips me when I see sandhill cranes
dancing in playas
their tracheal laughter contagious
as cloud seeding
or trampolines or an aria
for trombone
until I feel my own neck extending
inside which
mixed by turbulent diffusion
and cross-ventilation
a thermal rises, an updraft climbing
its pillar of air warmed by equivocal
sunlight, strafed by crows
and radio waves bouncing off
the Heaviside layer so that
even in Othello, Washington
I sense a tension like the hundred
thousand fist-sized bolts
of the Eiffel Tower straining
against a North Atlantic squall,
a low-pressure system
which began in an aerosol can
or as a mild disagreement
on a honeymoon in the tropics or the courtship
nosedive of an Anna's hummingbird
near the Gulf of California:
in this heady mood

when auroras ignite the ionosphere
like static electricity combing your hair
it's hard to steer clear
of the opportune meteor
punctuating the mesopause,
hard to miss the noctilucent clouds
shivering thin skinned and limbless
above the stratosphere
exuding its blue halo
like a conspicuous wish,
harder still to distinguish among
the many words misspoken
at the boundary layer—
all guff and stammer, bluff
and recrimination
mingling with excess
CO_2 emissions
to condense as particles of ice
at the tropopause
where the periodic sentence breaks—
the cold trap without which
no word would turn over
fall back to earth
as alpine snow,
rain filling the playas,
headwaters brimming a jar.

Notes & Acknowledgments

"The Changeling," "Among the Cypresses (23 Remedies)," and "The Break" are for Anaïs Charlotte. "Carousel" is for Thomas Craft. "Matinee" is for Ruth Mary Vieth.

"Les Calanques" refers to several narrow, fjord-like limestone fissures near Cassis, France. The poem alludes to the now underwater Cosquer Cave, as well as aubades written by Adam Zagajewski and Jennifer Grotz.

The passages in italics in "Wilson's Warbler" are taken from the letters of Alexander Wilson, and from his first recorded description of this now eponymous species (which he himself called a "Green Black-capped Flycatcher") in *American Ornithology*, the nine volumes of which (published 1808–1815) precede Audubon's more famous work and represent the first detailed scientific and literary treatment of American birds. In fact, as his biographers note, *American Ornithology* was "the first major scientific work wholly produced and published in the United States." Part 3 of this poem, which condenses details of Wilson's life, owes a special debt to *Alexander Wilson: The Scot Who Founded American Ornithology*, by Edward H. Burtt and William E. Davis.

"The Beardsley Limner" was an itinerant painter active in New England in the late eighteenth / early nineteenth century. His or her identity remains unknown.

"Linear A" and "Linear B" were inspired by images and pottery containing fragments of these ancient scripts, which I first saw in Crete.

"Persona Non Grata" was instigated by a line from Paul Valéry: *"Le lion est fait de moutons assimilés"* (A lion is assimilated sheep), from *Tel Quel*, 1943.

"Carmen Saeculare" is a departure from Horace's poem of the same title, and is for Carmen Zelaya, first and last on my life list.

"Old Paradox" refers to the classical "sorites paradox," or "paradox of the heap," which evokes the fluidity of boundaries in language as in nature.

In "Accidentals," part 1 describes a Neolithic votive figure found on Lipari; part 2 describes the scrolls found in the Villa dei Papiri in Herculaneum, and several methods used to unravel and read them, most recently X-ray phase contrast imaging, which in its early stages has yielded the phrases quoted in the last line. Beyond firsthand observation, this poem was inspired by, and borrows from, the reports of John Seabrook in the *New Yorker* and Victoria Jaggard in *Smithsonian*.

*   *   *

Grateful acknowledgment is made to the editors of the following journals and reviews, in which these poems first appeared, sometimes in earlier versions and under different titles:

The Account: Untitled #10; Persona Non Grata
The Adroit Journal: Therefore Wander
Alaska Quarterly Review: Les Calanques; On Turning 38 in Rome
Bellingham Review: Parents
Beloit Poetry Journal: Low Hanging Fruit
Calamaro: God: A Study
The Collagist: Utilitarianism; Entanglement (Satellite)
Copper Nickel: Among the Cypresses (23 Remedies)
The Far Field: Pigeon Guillemots
Green Mountains Review: Linear A; Lignum Vitae
The Hopkins Review: Finesse
Kenyon Review: The Changeling
The Laurel Review: An Illustrated Guide to Feathers
The Los Angeles Review: The Descent
The Monarch Review: Found Art; House Finch in Bird Bath
New Delta Review: Bivalve Lullaby

New England Review: One Atmosphere

Okey-Panky: Borders without Doctors; Carousel; Matinee

Poetry: For the Climbers; Figure of Aeolus

Poetry Northwest (David Biespiel, editor): New Volunteer at the Art Museum; Linear B; Carmen Saeculare

Prairie Schooner: Fuzz

Southern California Review: Flash Drive

Southern Humanities Review: Little Big Chief; The Break

SRPR: Entanglement (Sombrero)

Terrain.org: Wilson's Warbler (5)

Washington State Geospatial Anthology: Nisqually Delta

West Branch: Small Government

"On a Friday" was first published in the *Jack Straw Writers Anthology*, May 2008.

"Lignum Vitae" was reprinted in the *Green Mountains Review,* 25th Anniversary Poetry Retrospective, June 2012.

"Vagrants" was first published in the Pacific Poetry Project's *Alive at the Center* anthology, Ooligan Press, April 2013.

"Small Government" was republished on *Verse Daily*, and reprinted in *At the Water's Edge*, an anthology of the Skagit River Poetry Festival, May 2014.

"Pigeon Guillemots" was reprinted as a broadside for the Skagit River Poetry Festival, May 2016.

*   *   *

Written over a period of ten years or so, this book bears the imprint of many friends, and harbors many conversations distilled. The poems themselves are vessels of my gratitude. For editorial camaraderie, counsel, and encouragement, I would especially like to thank Linda Andrews, David Baker, Rick Barot, William Bernhard, David Biespiel, Michael Collier, Olena Kalytiak Davis, Sonia Greenfield, James Hoch, Rebecca Hoogs, Johnny Horton, Rod Jellema, Richard Kenney, Rachel Kessler, Brandon Krieg, Julie Larios, Dan Lamberton, Carol Light, Erin Malone,

Tod Marshall, Bryan Miller, Sierra Nelson, Colleen O'Brien, Katharine Ogle, Stanley Plumly, Bethany Reid, Zach Savich, Don Share, Martha Silano, Ed Skoog, G. C. Waldrep, Cody Walker, Kary Wayson, Jason White, Jason Whitmarsh, Wendy Willis, Catherine Wing, and Andrew Zawacki. There are many others, my familiars: you know who you are.

I'm indebted to the Bogliasco Foundation, the Camargo Foundation, 4Culture, and Artist Trust for time and support. I also want to thank Everett Community College, whose ongoing enthusiasm for and support of the written arts in Snohomish County has enriched my life as a teacher and a writer. Warmest appreciation for the diligence and kindness of the editors and staff at the University of Washington Press—Nicole Mitchell, Whitney Johnson, Nancy Cortelyou, Katherine Tacke, Rachael Levay, Dustin Kilgore, and Caroline Knapp.

Immense gratitude to the artist Robert Hardgrave, as well, for the endlessly evocative cover image.

My deepest thanks to Linda Bierds, fellow hiker, for steadfast belief in my work.

About the Author

Author photo: Fat Yeti Photography

Kevin Craft is the author of *Solar Prominence,* selected by Vern Rutsala for the Gorsline Prize from Cloudbank Books (2005), and editor of five volumes of the anthology *Mare Nostrum* (Writ in Water Press 2004–2009). He is the director of the Written Arts Program at Everett Community College, and teaches in the University of Washington's Creative Writing in Rome Program. His work has been honored with awards and fellowships from Artist Trust, 4Culture, the MacDowell Colony, the Bogliasco Foundation, the Camargo Foundation, and the Bread Loaf Writer's Conference. Editor-in-chief of *Poetry Northwest* from 2009–2016, he now serves as the executive editor of *Poetry Northwest Editions.*